PEDREGOSA ST.

PEDREGOSA ST.

POEMS

ENID OSBORN

Sheila-Na-Gig Editions

ISBN: 978-1-962405-47-8
Library of Congress Control Number: 2025946356

Sheila-Na-Gig Editions
Russell, KY
Hayley Mitchell Haugen, Editor
www.sheilanagigblog.com

Acknowledgments

Thanks to journals and anthologies where these poems—or versions of them—previously appeared in print.

Art/Life: "Lost Shoe"
ASKEW: "Why I Did Not Cut My Hair"
Cholla Needles: "January Dawn"
rivertalk: "The Agitated Heart"
Salt: "A Spirited House," "Crow in Fog," "San Pascualito"
Santa Barbara Literary Journal: "Cul-de-Sac Stories" (partial),
    "Glory in August," "Lázaro," "Lost Shoe," "The
    Difference Between a Rat and a Ghost"
We Are All God's Poems Anthology (Unsolicited Press): "We
    Are All God's Poems"

Thanks

To my landlords and neighbors; to my darling husband, Jay; to poet Paul Willis for his keen eye and careful comments; to mentors, employers, teachers and dear friends who have supported my writing life.

Thanks to the house for refuge, for a place of belonging, character, dreams. Thanks to the doors I go in and out of.

Foreword

In January 1997, when my poetry began to coalesce, I sought a modest place where I could live alone, write, and compile books. To make a book of poems takes two parts writing, two parts editing and six parts dreaming. A place to dream—that is what the Pedregosa house has been for me.

Built at the turn of the century, the big Vic holds much history. It has its own moods, echoes, and architectural quirks. Only three doors from the railroad, the house seems in perpetual motion. Trains give these poems their rhythm.

Many poems describe my early years living here, when the neighborhood earned its bad reputation. The owners I first knew died. The house was sold, remodeled and repainted in 2022. Some vintage features were restored at that time. The cul-de-sac, once active territory for Westside gangs, gradually settled down. New multiple-family housing projects in the area created a rise in density and traffic.

Although the poems are based on my experiences, I have freely exercised creative license. Landlords and neighbors should not be held accountable for any of the goings-on described in these pages. The living conditions are—and always have been—very nice. The presence of rats is exaggerated.

Enid Osborn

Fall, 2025

Names have been changed, except for

—Jon Wilsher—
1938-1999

First neighbor,
Englishman,
fine artist, cat-lover,
keen observer

Contents

Foreword

I. Cul-de-Sac

Finding Number Three	15
Cul-de-Sac Stories	16
Corner Store	21
Smash Medallion	23
The Mean Lady Upstairs	25
Roses	26

II. Jon

Life in Miniature	29
The Agitated Heart	30
Wild Orchid	32
Marmite	34
Broken Teapot	35
Six Questions	36
Glory in August	38

III. Birds

To the Shy Oriole in My Palm Tree	41
Washingtonias	42
Crow in Fog	43
January Dawn	44
Clan of the White Crow	45
Praise for the Plain Bird	46

IV. Ghosts

New Neighbor	49
The Causal Arrow of Time	50
Floating Shoes	52

The Difference Between a Rat and a Ghost   53
One Rat Theory   55
The Difference Between a Ghost and a Hermit   56
San Pascualito   58

V. Heaven

What Is Offered   61
Impermanence   62
Paradise   63
Arabella   65
We Are All God's Poems   66
Folding   67
Blessing of the Saint   68

VI. Awake

Lost Shoe   73
Lázaro the Painter   75
Manes of Pegasus   77
Why I Did Not Cut My Hair   78
Hair Storm   80
Books to Save   81
A Spirited House   82
Awake on the Westside   84
Mission Onramp   87

About the Author

I. Cul-De-Sac

Finding Number Three

Old Gino stops halfway up the stairs
to catch his breath. A ring of keys
dangles from his right hand.

He opens Number Three, crosses
to a pair of tall windows, grabs a long pole
and draws back the blinds.
Hope you like lots of light.

The room is tall. It is pristine.
Still, as though holding its breath.
From his perch on the sill,
Gino watches her pace.

Here she will sleep. Here she will read.
Here she will write at her desk. Or there.
Out the side door, a wide balcony to hold
pots of lavender and scented geraniums.
A narrow sunroom for asanas.
Here she will paint. A big bathroom,
a claw-footed tub. Here she will float.

At the southeast window, a giant eucalyptus.
At north-facing windows, trains and foothills.
At the kitchen sink, a mountain view.
Tidy, scalloped cupboards. Curious extra door.
For the iceman, says Gino. *You like old houses?*
This one's over a hundred.

She and the house exhale together.
Good bones, she says.
How soon can I move in?

Cul-De-Sac Stories

1

El Tigre throws brown bottles.
Boof-boof-boof.
Sixteen this morning.
Compacted, his glass fills
one large barrel a week.
It takes two strong garbage men
to roll it to the curb.

2

The freight creaks to a slow amble.
A screen door slams at the last house,
a man jumps the chain links, hits the side
of a rusted boxcar, and swings butt-first
through the half-open door.

Sometimes the freight stops
for twenty minutes, an hour,
giving Amtrak the right of way.

The woman who paints La Virgen
comes down from Mission Bridge
and picks out a green boxcar.
She unpacks her stencil.

Neighbors returning from market
pause beside the tracks
to watch La Virgen take form.
Children whisper. No one talks aloud.

Paint dries on sun-warmed metal.
As the train creaks and begins to roll,

the painter walks alongside,
putting up the last stars.

3

El Portero rakes the asphalt clean.
Not just the street in front of his house,
but the whole round of the cul-de-sac.

Half an hour of scratching each morning
we take for granted, like Mission bells.
The points on his rake are worn to nubs.

The Railroad builds a fence at the base
of the cul-de-sac to keep drug runners
from hopping the trains.

His side of the fence is clean.
On the other side, trash
crawls up the chain links.

4

Lion Dog makes his rounds
at a jaunty tick,
swinging his broad head down
on every plug and post.

He does not growl at strangers
or unfurl his tight plume
to greet a neighbor.

He ignores cats and avoids that
half-chow bitch at the last house.
They had a thing. That's all it was.

Mornings and evenings, he makes his rounds.
Afternoons, he lies on the warm asphalt
in front of his house, like a perfect sphinx.

Nothing raises his hairs except the Harleys—
Lion Dog cringes away from the sound
of glass packs as El Tigre pulls up
across the street and swipes the kickstand.

Three children pour out of the house,
crying *Daddy-Daddy!* To settle a dispute,
he smacks all three.

5

La Reina comes home from the graveyard shift,
parks her Caddy on the oil-soaked cement
and sways to her front door while her shih tzu

chuckles and throws himself against
the other side. He dances across the carpet
on hind feet while she puts up her things

and falls into the recliner. She has three
blooming granddaughters and a lover
from Oaxaca. Young *vato* hits her

when he drinks and, while she works,
he locks the dog in the bathroom
where he cries for help.

After a night like this, there is no discernible
difference in the greeting the dog gives her.
Perhaps more dancing.

6

Gino's a kind old man, waiting
for his cat to come home.
Have you seen my Lily?

Emphysema's got him by the short hairs.
Used to be a looker, now he's thin as a rail,
coughing up lung in mighty heaves,

bags under his eyes big as testicles.
Don't make him laugh, unless you want
his death on your head.

After a party in Number One, he picks
a pair of rubber titties from the grass
and models them for Reina and me,
rolling his skinny old hips in a hula.

7

The man on the corner grumbles
as he goes up and down the ladder
to trim his ten-foot, wrap-around hedge.

He vows to move away, leave the neat
white house with its stone walk
and raised vegetable garden.

While he works,
his old, white-faced retriever stands
half-in, half-out of the hedge,
waiting pleasantly for passersby.

Inside the hedge, her tail wags.
The man cannot ask her to move
someplace new.

8

In the evening, neighbors walk
to and from the corner store,
filling their water jars.

Greetings are exchanged
in four languages.
They pause together
at the first rose garden
and point to a thin yellow moon.

Corner Store

Cho smokes, leans on the steel railing
at the entrance to Mission Liquor.
The sign says, "No shoes, no entry."

He smokes with that James Dean air
of tragedy, though he is forty,
Korean-American, and his taciturn

cloud is darker than any *baeg-in*
could possibly muster, even one who has
made a pact to die young. His face,

remarkably handsome, rarely cracks.
If he saw her approach, if she smiled in greeting,
he would not smile back, bet your money.

She is a neighborhood regular. Still,
she doesn't rate a greeting. Same routine
for fifteen years: *Hi.* No answer.

Sometimes she says, *Have a good day,*
as she sweeps up her bag of goods.
Once, five years ago, he muttered,
You, too, my friend.

Another rare conversation
was prompted by a compliment she made
on his vintage T-shirt collection.

Another day—and keep in mind
these exchanges were years apart—
she said, *There's a man in the parking lot.*

A panhandler. His hands are bleeding.
He vaulted the counter and went outside.
You have to leave. You can't do this here.

She listened just inside the door.
The man began to protest, *But—*

You have to leave. Now. Or I call the cops.
Cho stood with his feet apart
and watched until the man
disappeared around the corner.

The following week, Cho
rang up her chips and vinegar.
He said, *Did you hear about*
that suicide on the tracks?
Right over here? he pointed.
Do you think it was that young man?
The one with the hands?

She did not reach for her bag.
Could be, she said. *If so,*
I am sorry for him.
To be so hopeless.

Yes, Cho said, *so am I.*

Smash Medallion

Every adept is a survivor of despair.

1

The faces of Mary, Claire and Martín
shine from the rail in vague
and misshapen rapture.

They gaze up for hours,
lasting out the day of trains.

At dawn, they held themselves flat,
magnetized against the lurching rail,
waiting for the moment of impact,
the moment they would be set free.

The rail, still warm, bears the stamp
of three glittering ovals, their delicate images
laid over the pocked and polished steel.

This rail, this kneeling bench,
lights up at daybreak like pink neon,
the road of fire
as good a road to heaven as any.

2

She bends to pick among
the crushed and sooty rocks, spray cans,
condoms, broken glass,
looking for a crust of cheap nickel alloy,
dearer than money.

She wants to know the speed,
the warp of the wheel,
the degree of heat that shape
and guide the flight of the vessel,
its velocity, what distance it flies
and in what direction,

whether it bounces, skips, or lodges
among the rocks, whether it hatchets
the split, oil-soaked beam
or, to her delight, lies bright and easy
upon the surface, reflecting sky.

There is no science but wonder.
If you were a ruined saintscoat,
which way would you fly?

A hunch may lead her to it. If not, she spends
an hour—or all the time it takes—to make
this recovery. She circles the marked place,
kneels at the rail, paces off the beams,
scans the broken rocks.

3

The moment she sees the tiny glint of metal,
her breath is suspended. In that moment
before her hand shoots out, God chuckles.

She turns the scrap like an oracle piece,
holds it to light, measures the warp and shear
with her sooty thumb, then,
loving its secret life and death,
bears it home to another altar.

On the days when she fails to recover,
she is consoled by—and carries bright in mind—
that gossamer image stamped upon the rails
in the shape of a perfect oval, emitting
its own light, like a brief visitation,

the upturned face of a saint,
damaged and set free.

The Mean Lady Upstairs

She got that face by disapproving
of the neighbors, the ones who
smoked up the hallway
and siphoned her electricity.

The ones who dripped paint
on the sidewalk, left their wardrobe
at the curb, parked two cars
in one allotted space.

The ones whose vicious dogs
ran loose in the street, killing
smaller dogs and cats
and crapping in her driveway.

It was she who sicced the pound on the dogs
and she who called the cops when the
downstairs neighbor bounced his girlfriend
against the wall. And, in case you wondered,

it was she who ratted you out to the landlord
and circulated a petition to get rid of you.

The Mean Lady used to have a lovely garden
with a statue of Mary and red geraniums
dripping down but that didn't do much
for her image, did it?

Mary took a BB to the head and the garden
withered to skeletal vines. Children speed up
when they ride their scooters under her perch,
asking dear, brain-damaged Mary

to hide them from the Mean Lady's radar.
Curious faces look back for a glimpse
and sometimes catch her on the balcony,
bending to water her cactus.

Roses

She has a passion for roses,
tries to grow a bush in a pot.

Not just any bush, but one
capable of fighting back.

Punctures are bad for gloves.
Barehanded, she oils the dark leaves.

Fish and bone, peace.
Bowl of water, peace.

She hums as she buries her gifts.
A bit of mildew, aphid, rust may live.

She likes to think Compassion
is a woman floating backward,

away from the flickering blue light
of the living room,

away from the super-white light
of the convenience store,

receding into a cloak of stars.
She likes to think this woman

floats above her roses at night
to receive their exhalations of love.

II. Jon

Life in Miniature

Jon paints and smokes,
paints and smokes,
dashes off oils of his neighbor,
his neighbor's bike,
the eucalyptus blooms,
his cat preening at the window.

His world gets smaller
as the lease on his heart runs out.
There are more miniatures now
and the large canvas stands unfinished.

The brindle is not as sweet as
the one-eyed tabby, but she likes to
curl on his foot while he paints.

After tea, he loads his brush
for a still life, the hand
of an old lover in repose,
a remembered landscape.

The Agitated Heart

A heart fits well in a hand.
Even a small hand.
Even a large heart, like yours,
swollen from work and damage.

They separate the sternum,
pull you apart like a food bird.

What would you choose
if somebody came for yours?

Say you were a shy man, and hands
came reaching for your heart:
Would you choose love
or precision?

The hands you see through your eyelids
are covered in wax and they've
touched many hearts and they
talk about yours and they
talk about yours and they
pass it beating and they
pass it bleeding from hand to hand
and your heart pleads for its life.

How could it know, more than a wild bird,
who means to save it
and who means to kill it?

Deals are made with heart tailor, pulse taker,
tube layer, blood sucker, seller of sleep.
You see it all, but judgment is white white white.
You cannot speak or change a thing.

When you waken, you look down your nose
at the crooked seam. You are strangely calm,
even buoyant, as you receive
an accounting of the surgery.

But when you ask your heart,
your heart won't speak. It shudders
in its broken cage.

Mended, but not safe, it relives
the moment when the hands came.

Wild Orchid

Wild stems come out of you. I watch
your heart write its uneven scrawl
across the screen. One machine

goes off like a cuckoo. Nurses talk
without censure and nobody knocks.
We call it The Invasion.

In the afternoon, you smile wanly
and press your list into my hand.
I leave you propped in your regalia.

At home, I put an ear against your wall.
The lock sticks, the door swings lightly open.
Old catbox, burnt toast, and your recent

argument with death hang in the air.
I bat about, calling *kitty kitty,*
paw through drawers and leaning stacks:

Checkbook, electric bill, reading glasses.
I finger the list, read and reread it.
Your good, angular hand gives courage.

Cats ask questions like two-year-olds.
I rattle kibble, tell them *Jon sent me.*
One comes to the dish.
The other, your favorite, hisses.

Oversized pencil studies
litter sofa and floor.
I linger over the one of a woman
watering her cactus.

A few items on your list
will not be found.

Too tired to leave, I stand before
a wet canvas, counting tubes of paint
that curl upon your table.

Marmite

On the morning of your last day,
you pour Assam from a yellow teapot
then watch over the edge of your cup
as I bite into toast prepared with
a thin layer of Marmite.

Your eyebrows point upward
like little tents. *Perhaps it's an
acquired taste,* you say.

Broken Teapot

stuck to the floor
on dry, flattened wings
thin legs cricketlike
eyes pinched
earlobes blackened
clay lips parted
before word or wine
fingers sharply segmented
blue as Shiva
pigment spreads
unevenly down
from a ruptured heart

I conjure you twenty times
in your close kitchen
amid swirling blue linoleum
and shards of a yellow teapot

to believe your silence Roshi
I remember how still you did lie

Six Questions

1

I will take care of
your unfinished painting,
tired hat, gas bill,
cup of pennies,
overdue book,
folder of research,
shadeless lamp,
and the stool your cat used
to jump in and out the window.

You will answer six questions
by your journal, pencil study,
note in the margin,
store receipt,
unmailed letter,
and magazine clipping.

I am not ashamed
to look for you everywhere,
diving under your bed
to retrieve your lost passport
and articles of fame.

2

Careful to step around the place
where your heart stopped, I raise
your stained teapot over my head
and smash it proper while you clap.

Otherwise, you don't say much.
You don't wave from the window,

hum in the kitchen, rattle teacups,
answer your phone or scrape a chair.

You are not on the balcony
where your flowers
beg for water.

One thing that stays
is the smell of old smokes in the hall.
Oh, and I found your black hoody
hanging on the door with a five-spot
in the pouch. Cheers for the cuppa.

Glory in August

After the jacarandas lose their blooms,
flowering gums deck Pedregosa
in splashy reds and pinks.

Bees and hummingbirds
spin a living halo for each tree.

Jon sits on the balcony, painting
great pompoms of Chinese Red
against leaves of Kombu Green.

Woodpeckers crisscross the low sky,
shouting derision from palm
to phone pole to gum tree.

A single scrub jay perches
on the uppermost twig
to scold the cat. As light dims,

a shy oriole takes to the outer branch
to sing his one-note song. Too late.
Jon has closed his box of paints.

III. Birds

To the Shy Oriole in My Palm Tree

I hear your chit-chit in late afternoon
as you rustle the dry fronds
for string to mend your basket.

You make a pretty, scalloped flight
to the power line, give a whistle
for your sweet olive girl.

I hang at the gate,
wander tree to tree until
my neck aches from gawking.

How can a taxi-yellow bird
possess such reticence?

Little paint, saffron joy,
come out, come out!
I have waited an hour
for a second glimpse.

And when, at last, you clear the leaves,
the sun has gone behind the hill.
Your slender figure perches in silhouette.

I tell my heart a lie to ease its longing.
I tell my eye the brilliant bird is there!

Washingtonias

Long before they put up those
crackerbox units on the street,

the Big House presided
over a spacious corner lot and those
leggy palms of Beverly Hills fame
marched the property line.

The narrow drive, built for a Model A,
led back, a sentinel tree at either side.

There are only five left.
On windy days, they hiss,
thrash the sky, make like a pretzel,
throw giant fronds at the street.

They're a liability! the owner says.

But what if, I say. *What if the fronds
were swept away?*

Granted a pardon,
the Washingtonias still misbehave.

The morning after a storm,
I don gloves, sweep palm berries,
drag great fronds into piles.

Neighbor children run to help.

Crow in Fog

Dawn comes from no direction.
The sun has seen fit to begin the day
in mourning.

Fog roils in the cul-de-sac and rains
from trees in big, oily splats. I walk around
the edge of wetness, clean as cut cloth.

A single crow sits on the phone pole
and tolls like a sad alto bell.

She makes her body a pointed
thrust of sound, rocks deeply,
throws her voice into the nether.

Such effort could exhort the clan to air
but she is solo.

Her sad jazz fits my outlook
like a pair of black tights.

January Dawn

You fly, silent, from post to post,
wait for me to pass, then glide ahead.

Not a proper shadow; more like
negative space in the shape of a bird.

I relish the satiny sound of your wings.

You are not my death bird,
not pet, nor what I call friend.

I have captured your interest
in the idle month of the sun's low ebb.

Mid-winter: A crow is free
to pursue a hobby.

In spring, the raucous clan returns
and, noisiest of all, its young.

But for now, crow studies woman,
woman studies crow in silence.

I welcome your company, yours alone,
this January dawn, cold and lean.

Clan of the White Crow

Hear tell, there was once an all-white crow.
What we call white crows today
are harlequins—a few white feathers
mixed in with the dark.

I saw one glide under the boughs
of a silk oak on San Pascual. The bird
was quickly lost in dappled light.

Six checkered crows landed in a circle
in the parking lot of La Mesa Grocery.
Each bird wore its badge of white
in a different place. The crows
took turns bowing into the circle.

I saw one with two white tail feathers
on a phone pole. Another, with one
white shoulder, shouted from a fence.

Sightings are rare now, but old-time
Westsiders still talk about them,
turning their faces aside when they speak.

Looking into the eyes of a neighbor
when talking about a white crow
is like looking directly at the white crow

which you must never do.

Praise for the Plain Bird
California Towhee

the true early bird
toils in the dark-before-light
repeating her sharp chirp

unobtrusive as a sparrow
less songful nor shouting
behold comes the dawn

her one note trims my dream
so welcome to my heart
she may as well be that trumpeter

at midday I see her
brown and featureless
foraging under the rosemary

undaunted by my presence
she counts her seeds
one day I will follow

and find out where she rests
if ever she does

IV. Ghosts

New Neighbor

The student goes out early for class,
stays late at the library, leaves the light on
for sixteen hours just to make sure

the hallway is lit when he gets home.
The lady in Number Three watches
TV at night. The X-Files theme plays

over and over, whistling through the wall.
At two, she turns off her set,
comes into the hallway, kills the light

and says goodnight to the ghost
who sits on the top stair.
Someone's in my house.

Go home, Jon, she says.

The Causal Arrow of Time

Bedtime asserts a strangeness,
the transition from upright to lying down
a diminishment of the guard.

When all the house goes to sleep,
I begin my battle *against* sleep
and keep it up into the wee hours
when neck gives like warm tallow

and head nods into deep space
or, if standing, one knee gives way
and I fall like a length of timber.

Let's talk about things
that happen while one is asleep.
The clever rat has its way.
A ghost stands in the hall.

Shoes walk themselves
across the tired carpet
or crawl deeper under the bed.

Scraps of paper, meant to remind me,
fall from their postings and lodge
behind books that are busy
reading themselves aloud.

My mother, Disruption, visits
from her coma to knock over
a jar of honey. A Westside banger
whistles one note beneath the window.

A spigot drips into a cup
that overflows, and Master sits

at the foot of my bed
to quietly chide me. He and Jon

talk about their paintings.
I strain to hear their conversation
over loud orchestral music,
knowing all the while that

the causal arrow of time
moves in one direction.
The hours are fleeting,
unwatched, wasted.

At daybreak, I open to
terrible dread
and remain skeptical
well into morning—

the world I have just left
more loved than this one—

until I rise and wash,
until I strike a blue flame
beneath the glass kettle,
until the sky shows its shy light,

and I begin again to forget
and slowly embrace this world,
the one with closets of wool
and bells of silver.

Floating Shoes

The thudding sound I sometimes heard
upon waking was not the ghost—
though this does not rule out
the presence of the ghost—

nor was it the rat, nor was it my downstairs
neighbor preparing for bed after working
the night shift, nor was it the heavy crow
landing on my roof.

In fact, it was my two shoes floating
beside the bed, held aloft by my
dream state, that came un-suspended
and hit the floor *thump-thump*
as I began to wake.

The volume of the thuds
must have depended on the height
of the shoes in air.

I sometimes heard them
but fell back into a dream—
their touchdown then doubted
or forgotten at second waking—

but I did wonder
why my shoes were not lying
side by side as I had left them—
How careless!

Apologies to the ghost if I am telling this wrong.
Apologies to my neighbor.
Apologies to the rat.

The Difference Between a Rat and a Ghost

1

You are comfortable with
the pops and sighs of the old house,
one hundred years and counting.

Animals
make a different sound inside the walls
than droll house spirits do.

You think you hear intention—
stealth, perhaps—it brings your chi
right to the surface.

Not the sound a bodiless soul makes
to say hello or to offer
some dry and timely comment
on what you were just thinking.

You don't have to take my word for it,
says the ghost, laissez-faire as all get out.

The intruder, on the other hand,
is anything but ambivalent
and doesn't give a rat's ass
what you think.

He is alive
and wants to stay that way.

2

He climbs up the ancient skeleton
of abandoned plumbing inside the wall
toward a dim crescent of light
and the smell of neglect,

punches the powdery calking
with one hand, and squeezes through
into the lower cupboard, the one
you never clean, so as not to stir memories.

He is now officially trespassing,
a noble rat vocation,
and likes what he smells. He possibly
likes your kitchen more than you do.

The spaces you fail to inhabit
are neon signs, written in rat.

One Rat Theory

You thought she was too wily
to be caught with so little effort,
tail stretched out behind her
in all its naked length.

You do not question the rat
but believe at once in the rat's death,
though every tick and flutter you hear
in the old house, starting tonight,
will be a rat. Rat first, then a list

of alternate explanations.
A new rat, not the same rat.

But what if there is only ever one rat
and the death of that rat in your kitchen
and the ghost of that rat ever after?

You drift in and out of sleep as the rat
gnaws and rests, gnaws and rests.
Next day, you check the sticky trap
to find a dimple where one foot
set down and pulled away.

The Difference Between a Ghost and a Hermit

Not much difference. The hermit makes a rare
appearance downstairs. Neighbors are surprised
to see her. With each appearance, she looks older
than they remembered.

Occasionally, in the early evening, she stands
under a palm tree for minutes on end, looking up
as though waiting for something to appear.

Once, a policeman knocked on all the neighbors'
doors to ask if the woman in his photo was the
hermit. They looked and said they couldn't be
sure. *She pretty much keeps to herself,* they said.

Finally, the policeman came to the hermit's door.
There was a sign that read, "Please be quiet in the
hall." When he knocked, the hermit opened the door
a crack, then, seeing his uniform, stepped
into the hallway.

*Obviously, this is not a photo of me, but I do know
this woman,* the hermit said. She pointed to a drawing
of Buddha, framed and hung beside her door, and
said the woman in the photo had made it and given
it to her. *See? This is her signature.*

The lamp in the hermit's window goes off and on.
Well, a ghost could maybe do that.

The hermit shouts at rodents. She talks on Zoom or
on the phone or to herself. Recites a poem. Whistles.
Claps. Coughs. Strikes a singing bowl. Chops garlic.

Neighbors hear water in the pipes. They sometimes hear her TV in the wee hours if they are awake for some other reason, such as indigestion. Her volume is tuned to a whisper.

The hermit's car disappears from the lot for short periods. Her mail gets picked up every few days. Occasionally, somebody leaves food or flowers on the porch. She opens the door to take these in, but no one sees her do it.

San Pascualito

Don't stay too long
on the street of The Grave King.

You narrowly outlived your neighbor
by doing the monkey dance but now
Death has been inside your house.
He doesn't have to pick the lock.

Maybe you think you are immune
like that year in Albuquerque you lived
next to biker thieves and no one
dared to rob you. Do you suppose

The Grave King watches out for you
or just watches? On San Pascual
you get your wish to live
a nearly secret life.

While the neighbors party down
oblivious of their bony guest
you lock your roomful of saints
and slip out into the gray hour
hoping to go unnoticed.

V. Heaven

What Is Offered

Gino snoops in the neighbor's mailbox,
pulls up an envelope from so-and-so hotshot
oncologist—*aha*, he thinks—and watches
as she passes by the window, one-sided
and gimpy, carrying her stack of clean towels.

Next night, she arrives home in the rain.
He runs to her side to share a newspaper hat
and shouts, *Do you need money?*

Money, she says.

She is old around the eyes
and would look surprised by his offer
if anything could surprise her.
She shakes her head no.

Is there anything else you need?

Sleep, she says in a faraway voice.
I haven't slept in weeks.

Impermanence

She has constructed everything
out of paper and crafty sticks

Pictures peel off her walls at night
and haunt the house with their
soft fallings

She leaves them behind the bookshelf
Someone will find them with their
ghostly companions of lint

Friends whisper while her eyes are closed
She trains her ears to the heart's noise

Bad luck to hear one's own eulogies
no matter how kind

Paradise

1

This morning
as I drove to work
the sun's forehead
hit my windshield

and I passed through a white blind
for one maybe two seconds
hardly long enough for my foot
to let up on the gas

When the sun withdrew
and the precious world
filled my window once again
this was not a place I recognized

2

Tonight as I climbed
the long staircase to home
there was a spell where
the light from the landing above
and the light from the foyer
did not touch

I climbed in darkness
for two maybe three seconds
too brief a time
to misstep or even pause

Had the stair not risen
to meet my foot I might have
fallen through space as one

falls at the outset of a dream
not into the arms of some near earth
but into a new dimension

3

Tomorrow if I tell you
I am dying you will
smother me with love
don the velcro of regret
raise your prayers to heaven—
that heaven up there—

but you will forget
you will forget again
and on a day much too soon
curse me for a trifle

In time you will know
I tiptoed past while you
dozed in your chair
on my way to a dimension
briefly visited

I always knew paradise
was not above us

Arabella

There are many signs of beckoning
when a life is torn

I walk and fly through perfect holes
revealed at the last moment

Like a finch disappears into the eaves
Like a swift pierces the grey, soft lining
with her pointed wrists

I am suddenly through to the other side
and in this cold, fresh place
I speak your name.

We Are All God's Poems

implies he crafted us
or perhaps implies
he hears us

our prayers
and the true unutterable
poems of yearning

all my days
I look for signs of love
even as a small child

I studied the lay of sticks in dirt
believing that nothing—
not me not a stick—

was left to carelessness
the stutter of a moth at my ear
the wry tilt of a bird's head

the circling of dragonflies
the pause of a fox on her path
to look me calmly in the eye

I keep myself fit
to catch the gift
to bear it

still I wonder
when wild bluebirds
hop along the fence

as I barely at arm's length
sweep palm berries from the walk
what possesses them

Folding

The one washer-dryer
that serves four families
has finally stilled.

I fold towels late into the night,
match corners, smooth the face
of each nappy cloth.

My Teacher chants
this is trivial, this is not
until, like the machines,

I am quieted.
With my perfect stack
I float up the stairs,

mindful to step lightly
over the top stair,
the one that speaks.

Blessing of the Saint

> We possess nothing.
> All is given.
>   —Karunamayi

With a dab of cool paste
on the lid of my third eye I run
from her flowering presence

and go up the road
walking and falling
turning over like a leaf in wind

I come to a car in the ditch
as though some careless thief
had discarded it there

The engine will not start
but this is a hiccup
I roll the windows down

and drive as one pursued
through a five-mile corridor
of chanting trees

At the end I come to a tall house
I go in
The stairs do not protest

On the second floor
I enter a lighted room

There are soft clothes in the closet
of pleasing hue and weave
There is a little food on the shelf

I find a face cloth beside the basin
but not ready to wash away
the blessing of the saint

I lie down on the good bed
with my middle eye open
and cry tears of gratitude

for clean sheets
and the welcome they imply

VI. Awake

Lost Shoe

I wondered all day about a lost shoe
I saw in the middle lane

and a strange young man came to my door
with a tie on and a black book

and because the shoe was a black shoe
and this young man at my door looked so unsure

I dreamt *he* lost the shoe
and he still went door to door—

his foot touched the ground many times
and then he was better.

There's a pair of chucks slung by their laces
over a power line on San Andrés.

They fill up with water when it rains
and squirt from the rivets like those
statues of Mary that cry real tears.

One day the shoestrings will rot.
I drive under them each morning

and pray for them to fall on me
and kick my car.

If you lost a shoe it might hurt you,
if your brother got it in a scuffle

and threw it out the car window just as
you were calling him shithead,

or if you had a sore foot shaped like
a fish or an anvil, it might hurt.

What if the shoe was too big
or it broke and just fell off like that

teeny white plastic maryjane I saw
in the leaves—

I swear, that shoe followed me
all over the Westside.

What if she needed to run?
There's glass everywhere.

Be careful.

Lázaro the Painter

Lázaro the painter sings a corrido
on the stairs, where the ceiling is high
and boomy. He hams it up, mariachi-style,

as he rolls out the primer coat—
the layer that boosts the final coat,
allowing the color to shine true.

Lázaro bears the name of a man
who, entombed in darkness, was called forth
to demonstrate the rewards of faith.

Even a dead man may balk at such
an offer, may choose to remain
in a world dark and now familiar.

But Lazarus emerges and walks
into the arms of a stranger with a voice
seductive as living water.

Indeed, his first view of new life
quivers behind a veil of tears,
his brain doubting more than ever
what his eyes tell him to be true.

A painter's life is truth—
trueness of color—
no guesswork involved,
each recipe exact as a baker's.

He falls in love as he fingers the sample,
again as he pries open the can.

This house will be the shade
of winter squash. Red for the doors
like blood of the bull.

Not your prim old lady, this,
but a male Vic—square,
with strong cornices.

Under the high eaves, Lázaro clings
like a spider, reaching to accent
sill and curlicue with expert stroke,
the size and hair of the brush
chosen for each detail.

In the morning, he sings on the stairs.
In the afternoon, he sings in the sky.

Manes of Pegasus

What she loved about that apartment
on the second floor of a creaky old Vic
beside the railroad tracks

with the ancient bathtub and drippy fixtures,
especially in winter when a cold draft
came through the ill-fitted windows, was

washing her hair in a big slope-ended tub,
perched high on lion's toes.

The sun climbed through the south-facing
window at nine and filled the bathroom
with light. Even if the water was tepid,

the steam in that bright, cold sunlight
was furious! furious! When she raised
her dripping hands, they emanated

a wild aura: Two players in the pantheon,
backlit and mighty, with flowing
manes and tails. They were dark suns,

dancing in the heavens. They were
twin heralds of a coming age.
She shivered before them.

Why I Did Not Cut My Hair

Because each follicle is a tiny antenna
and the longer the antennae, the more
intelligence I can collect.

Because I kept my hair all the way through cancer.
Because I kept my hair all the way through
menopause, though I shed like a dog
who was left in the car.

Because hair wants to do its own thing.

Because the arbiters of fashion
say *Cut it short after forty*
and the gravitational pull of planets
at the moment of my birth caused
a lifelong tendency to act contrary
to expectation.

Because the *abuelitas* in my neighborhood
sport braids down to their waists that swing
when they walk.

Because Frida cut hers to spite an unfaithful man,
and I, who have no unfaithful man, am grateful.

Because those Native American boys who were
recruited to scout during wars
lost their uncanny abilities
after they were given the buzz cut.

Because my husband used to tousle
my short curls and now
he watches my hair with a sort of shyness.

Because long hair flies in wind
and floats like seaweed.

Because it catches the eastern light
to make a kind of halo.

Because hair is a holy garment.

Hair Storm

It surprised her, this decision
coming down from the head
like a clandestine cloud-seeding.

Hair began to fall, at first in a series
of short bursts. Later, when soaked,
it fell in cabbages of pure white.

I am dying, said a voice.
I am paying for my sins. Both things
true but having little to do with hair.

It clung to the back of the velvet loveseat,
carpeted the carpet like a collie's undercoat.
Hair in the soup, hair in the door screen.

She could do nothing to hold it,
lost more hair than she should have
possessed. And with it, memories flew.

Each strand took a name, a place where
she once had lived, a road to home.
Random facts and their order: disremembered.

She swept it up, knotted it, spun it into yarn,
coiled it inside a seashell like ear fluff,
made a pillow for Little Buddha,

hung it on a nail for songbirds
to line their nests with—it moved
in the breeze like a living thing.

The birds would have none of it
but changed their flight path
to avoid its weird dance.

Books to Save

Thomas Fire, Santa Barbara, December 2017

Lighting the ridge, a mane of flames
heads toward the city.
If the heroes can't stop it,
it'll make of Mission Street a bright canyon

prepared to evacuate at a moment's notice.
I make a pile of books in the center of the room.
If I think I can re-buy the book, I leave it on the shelf.

We will find each other again, I say to William,
Mary, Pablo, Rainer, Rumi, Sylvia, and gingerly pick
slim volumes, one-off anthologies kind enough
to take my poems and nestle them in.

And the books by you, my friends,
precious volumes my hands longed to hold
years before they sprang into the world
to be showered with praise.

These are the books I choose to save.

This house that gave me shelter
I will leave some day for some reason—
a fire, a quake, a weariness of climbing stairs,
a change of ownership, a whim.

From my eastern window I watch Thomas
jump the ridge and travel downhill
toward the heart of town. This path
will likely bring fire to our threshold.

The wind will do the rest.

A Spirited House

> One need not be a Chamber – to be Haunted
> One need not be a House –
> The brain has Corridors – surpassing
> Material Place –
> —Emily Dickinson

Sometimes she surprises her younger self
on the stairs, or as she waters plants on the balcony,
roots in the closet for lost boots,
sets a vase of tulips on the nightstand.

Only now, as she begins to pack, does she
understand the house was never haunted.

It was her older self who watched,
who clucked her tongue and made
the stairs creak with her footfall.

She who ticked her impatience inside the walls,
flickered the lights, cried out in a dream.

She who, trapped in the crawlspace,
went mad from desire, hoarded and displaced
photos, cooked dry the Pyrex percolator
and said goodbye to the last generation
of orioles in the Washingtonia.

The handprints on the windowsill—
those were hers, too.

She lingered beyond reason.
At last, the many stairs became a steep ladder.

She arrived breathless at Door #3, which swung
open to a room she hardly recognized.

I think I used to live here, she said,
repeating the very words the ghost had said to her
thirty years before.

Awake on the Westside

At three a.m. a lamp burns in the cul-de-sac
and, in the quiet, a single voice may be heard—

the rude downshift of a semi, the hiss of a rusted
 owl in the palm, the scratch of a pen on dry paper.

At four, a train wails at the station two miles away.
The sound builds in the night, four engines straining

with a full load behind. A searing white light
sweeps the shallow canyon between road bank

and houses. Gaining speed, the train barrels past
Pedregosa, squeals, hisses, slams the tracks

and lumbers over Mission Bridge. The old Vic
jitterbugs, empty chairs walk, china sings atop

the shelves, a crack in the wall grows wider.
This house, a bare thirty yards from the tracks,

knows much about trains. At five o'clock,
the asphalt lies cool on Micheltorena Bridge.

Golden lamps cast fixed shadows—no rolling cars
to xerox, no can pickers, no workers on bikes,

no women on their way to market, no stray dogs,
only the little bats whose shadows flit

like doubts one may choose to ignore.
Just before the streetlamps extinguish,

those bigger doubts, the crows, begin
their journey across the sky. At first,

they speak little and pass for black
but one green crow—a parrot—flies among

and shrilly mimics the crows' speech.
Several more are not strictly black, but descendants

of the Westside White Crow, random streaks
and patches of white on their wings, as if,

on an errand of mischief, they flew beneath
a rain of paint.

Blue gum eucalyptus, night jasmine,
pittosporum mingle their oils with a mist

of fish and tar. The boys who vault the chain link
fence are not Westside Lokos, just boys

in bleached t-shirts who jostle for position
as they wind their way home along the tracks.

The old woman stands at her stove, heating coffee.
Her heavy braid falls to her waist.

A boy comes in, closes the door softly.
¿A dónde fuiste? ¿Qué hiciste?

I'm tired, abuelita, he says. *Déjame.*
And he falls asleep in his clothes,

resting on his belly, once again
the child she knows.

As the freeway finds its sure and even tides,
the boy dreams. The poet carefully presses

her pages, throws off the afghan,
shuffles to the kitchenette,

lights a blue flame under the pot,
greets the mountain that stands

in her window, and the morning becomes
a sink of dishes, a pair of shoes, the daily news,

and a clock on the wall that tells her when
it's time to catch the One-O-One.

Mission Onramp

Summer fog
morning rush hour

Pigeons line up
equidistant on the long arm
of a streetlamp

Drivers at the light
forget to gun their engines
The underpass is muted

Everything flows
in slow motion
birds
cars
the city sprinkler
that sprays each driver
on the entrance ramp

hush-hush-hush

This is how it should be
A slow beginning
a gentle shower
the smell of a new wet road

About the Author

Enid Osborn is a 45-year resident of Santa Barbara, California, and served as the city's Poet Laureate in 2017-2019. *Pedregosa St.*, Osborn's second full-length book of poetry, takes place in an upper Westside neighborhood of Santa Barbara.

Her first book, titled *When the Big Wind Comes* (Big Yes Press, 2015), describes her childhood in Southeast New Mexico, where her family raised quarter horses. Her poems appear mainly in West Coast and Southwest journals and anthologies. Her poem "The Place of Loss" was nominated by *Askew* for a Pushcart Prize. With Yucca Valley poet Cynthia Anderson, she co-edited *A Bird Black as the Sun: California Poets on Crows & Ravens,* featuring the work of 81 poets, living and bygone (Green Poet Press, 2011.) www.enidosbornpoet.com

Sheila-Na-Gig Editions